D1243414

Learning About the Circulatory and Lymphatic Systems

by John C. Gold

Enslow Publishers, Inc.
40 Industrial Road
Box 398
Berkeley Heights, NJ 07922
USA

http://www.enslow.com

In memory of Robin Provost Walker

Original edition published as *The Circulatory and Lymphatic Systems* in 2004.

Library of Congress Cataloging-in-Publication Data:

Gold, John Coopersmith.
  Learning about the circulatory and lymphatic systems / John C. Gold.
      p. cm. — (Learning about the human body systems)
  Summary: "Learn amazing facts about the Circulatory and Lymphatic Systems and discover how
they work together to keep us alive"— Provided by publisher.
Includes bibliographical references and index.
  ISBN 978-0-7660-4156-1
  1. Cardiovascular system—Juvenile literature. 2. Lymphatics—Juvenile literature. I. Title.
  QP103.G652 2013
  612.1—dc23

                                                    2012011099

Future Editions:
Paperback ISBN 978-1-4644-0234-0
ePUB ISBN 978-1-4645-1153-0
PDF ISBN 978-1-4646-1153-7

Printed in the United States of America

082012 Lake Book Manufacturing, Inc., Melrose Park, IL

10 9 8 7 6 5 4 3 2 1

To Our Readers: We have done our best to make sure all Internet addresses in this book were active and appropriate when we went to press. However, the author and the publisher have no control over and assume no liability for the material available on those Internet sites or on other Web sites they may link to. Any comments or suggestions can be sent by e-mail to comments@enslow.com or to the address on the back cover.

✿ Enslow Publishers, Inc., is committed to printing our books on recycled paper. The paper in every book contains 10% to 30% post-consumer waste (PCW). The cover board on the outside of each book contains 100% PCW. Our goal is to do our part to help young people and the environment too!

Photo Credits: ©Life Art, Williams & Wilkins, pp. 4, 6, 9, 11, 15, 18, 21, 38; © Photodisc, p. 25; Scott Camazine/ Photo Researchers, Inc., p. 36; Shutterstock.com, pp. 1, 22, 30, 41; © Susan Dudley Gold, pp. 17, 26.

Cover Photo: Shutterstock.com

Contents

CIRCULATORY SYSTEM

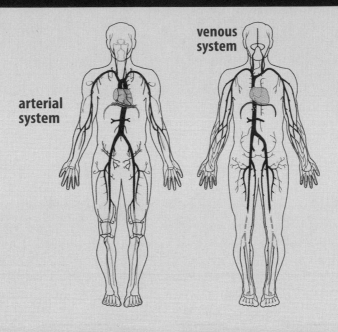

arterial system

venous system

LYMPHATIC SYSTEM

What Are the Circulatory and Lymphatic Systems?

Chapter 1

Think of the human body as a city bustling with highly coordinated activity. Within this city are many different systems, or service areas. Each of these areas has a specific job that is critical to the survival of the city.

For example, the body's skeleton creates the shape or structure. The muscles make the body move. The digestive system turns food into fuel that the body's parts can use to perform their tasks. The brain controls the whole show, and the skin provides protection for everything inside.

But in order for all these systems to do their job, they must have nutrients. They must have oxygen. And they've got to be able to get rid of the waste they create while doing their jobs.

Just like a giant highway, the **circulatory system** brings oxygen and nutrients to the body's parts and removes waste products. The system's "roads"—a network of tubes called vessels—extend to every part of the body. These vessels carry blood and other liquids. The delivery trucks—blood **cells**—carry oxygen to every part of the body. The blood cells also remove waste products.

A picture of the circulatory system looks like a street map of a city. There are many types and sizes of vessels. The largest vessels lie in the center of the body. As the vessels extend to other parts of the body, they grow smaller and smaller.

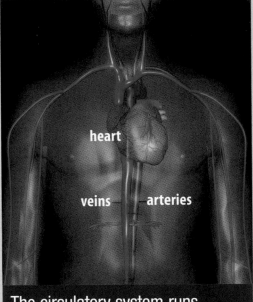

The circulatory system runs through the body like a system of roads. At the center, the heart provides the power for the system.

Vessels take blood from the center of the body. Other vessels bring the blood back to the center of the body. A pump called the **heart** moves the blood.

Another network of vessels, the **lymphatic system**, helps control the amount of liquid in the body.

This is the story of the heart, its vessels, and the lymphatic system and how they work together to keep us alive.

Working Together

Chapter 2

The circulatory system has three major parts:

1) a network of vessels that reach out to every part of the body;
2) blood and other fluids that circulate in the vessels (these fluids carry oxygen and fuel to the cells and remove waste products); and
3) the heart, a pump that moves these fluids through the network of vessels.

Blood vessels are tubes with several different layers. These layers give the tubes great strength and also allow them to stretch as pressure in them grows and shrinks with every heartbeat. The inside layer, called the **tunica intima**, is made of flat, very smooth cells. These help the blood flow smoothly through the vessel. The middle layer is the thickest and strongest. This is called the **tunica media**. The outside layer is called the **tunica adventitia**. This layer contains nerves and tiny blood vessels that bring oxygen and nutrients to the larger blood vessel.

There are two major kinds of blood vessels: **arteries** and **veins**. Arteries are the largest and strongest. They carry blood away from the heart to all the cells in the rest of the body. This blood is loaded with oxygen and nutrients that the cells need. Arteries must be strong because they receive blood that is pumped directly from the heart. The force of the blood causes the artery to expand, just like a bicycle tire does when air is pumped into it.

The arteries nearest the heart are the largest. The **aorta**, which is attached to the heart, is the largest blood vessel in the body. It is about one inch in diameter.[1] As the arteries get farther from the heart, they get smaller, like branches on a tree. And like tree branches, the arteries split off in many different directions. The smallest arteries, called **arterioles**, are so narrow that red blood cells must pass through them in single file.[2]

By the time an artery reaches the end of its route, it has become very, very small. Its three layers have become a single layer of cells.[3] These tiny vessels are called **capillaries**. Capillaries look like a very fine net. Their thin walls allow oxygen and nutrients in the blood to flow out of the vessel and into nearby cells. The thin walls also allow waste products from the cells to flow into the vessels.

Once the blood has delivered oxygen and nutrients to the cells and picked up waste products, it passes through the capillaries into the veins. Veins are not as strong as arteries because they do not receive the full force of blood being pumped by the heart. The veins carry the blood back to the heart and the lungs.

Veins have valves that help keep the blood moving toward the heart in a one-way circuit. These valves prevent the blood from flowing backward.

Blood Cells

If blood vessels are the body's highway, then blood cells are the trucks that travel the road. These cells help transport oxygen to other cells. They also provide protection from invaders and help repair damage to the circulatory system.

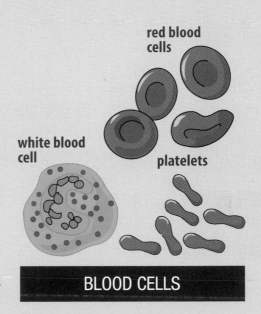

There are three kinds of blood cells. The most numerous are red blood cells, known as **erythrocytes**. There are 25 trillion erythrocytes in the body.[4] Red blood cells live between 80 to 120 days. When they die, new cells made in the bone marrow replace them. Bone marrow is living material inside the bone.

Red blood cells are important because they carry oxygen to other cells. They do this with the help of a protein called **hemoglobin**. This protein contains iron and can capture tiny particles, or molecules, of oxygen. Hemoglobin proteins that contain oxygen make red blood cells red. When hemoglobin molecules don't contain oxygen, red blood cells are blue. This is why veins look blue, because they are carrying blood that doesn't have any oxygen—it has already been delivered to the body's cells.

White blood cells detect and fight viruses, bacteria, and other foreign invaders. There are several kinds of white blood cells, each with a different task. Some types attack foreign invaders such as bacteria and viruses by surrounding and digesting them. Other white blood cells clean up dead or damaged body cells.

Still another kind of white blood cell makes proteins that help the body remember infections it has fought in the past. These proteins, called **antibodies**, let the body respond more quickly when the same infection enters the body again. Some white blood cells leave the circulatory system to help other parts of the body fight infections. White blood cells live from a few days to a few months.

The third kind of blood cells are platelets, also called **thrombocytes**. These act as the circulatory system's repair crew. When a blood vessel is damaged, these cells clump together at the site. This activity is called clotting, and it causes wounds to stop bleeding. Platelets live for about nine days before they are replaced.

Blood cells move through the circulatory system in a liquid called plasma. Plasma is mostly water, but it also contains minerals, nutrients, and proteins that the body needs.

The Heart

The heart keeps everything moving. This amazing muscle is about the size of a small grapefruit and beats about seventy times a minute when the body is resting. It beats constantly, twenty-four hours a day.[5]

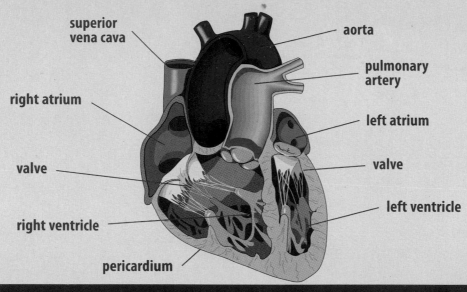

superior vena cava

aorta

pulmonary artery

right atrium

left atrium

valve

valve

left ventricle

right ventricle

pericardium

THE HEART

The heart has four chambers. It is divided into two halves, the right and the left. On top of the heart are the right **atrium** and the left atrium. These smaller chambers collect blood from the rest of the body. Together, these two chambers are called atria.

Below the atria are the right **ventricle** and the left ventricle. These larger and stronger chambers have thick, muscular walls and are responsible for pumping blood out of the heart and into the rest of the body through the arteries.

Between each heart chamber is a one-way valve. These valves keep the blood flowing in one direction through the heart. The valves are made from flaps, or cusps, that move in one direction only. Blood flowing to the right pushes the flaps open. Blood that tries to flow backward causes the flaps to close.

A tough sac called the **pericardium** surrounds the heart. This sac is filled with fluid that helps protect the heart.

The Lymphatic System

Working beside the circulatory system is the lymphatic system. This is a network of tubes called lymphatic vessels. The lymphatic system helps move excess fluid from the body's tissues into the circulatory system. This network is also an important part of the body's immune system.

Lymphatic vessels are larger than capillaries but smaller than the smallest veins. Like veins, they have one-way valves. These valves keep fluid in them moving away from the body's tissues and into the circulatory system. Lymphatic vessels are found in nearly every tissue and body organ that has blood vessels.

The fluid in the lymphatic system is called **lymph**. Lymph is a thick, pale liquid, similar to the plasma in blood. It contains fats and large numbers of white blood cells. At many points along the lymphatic network, the vessels widen and swell to resemble small beans. These areas are called **lymph nodes**. These nodes are sometimes called lymph glands, but this is not a correct term. The nodes are filled with a mesh-like tissue that helps to filter foreign particles from the lymph. Lymph nodes have their own blood supply.

After passing through the lymphatic system, lymph flows into two large ducts or tubes, the **thoracic duct** and the right lymphatic duct. These ducts return lymph to the circulatory system through large veins near the neck.

How Do the Systems Work?

Chapter 3

Human beings are made from millions of microscopic structures called cells. These are like tiny factories, each with a specific job. Some make chemicals that help to digest food. Others move messages from the brain to various parts of the body.

Cells group together to do certain jobs. For example, the cells in the liver are designed to help clean the blood. The cells in the skin work to shield the inner body from harm. In order to do their jobs, these cells require fuel. The circulatory system delivers this fuel, in the form of nutrients and oxygen.

Start at the Heart

Every day, more than 2,000 gallons of blood moves through the circulatory system. During that time the blood picks up oxygen. Then the blood travels to the cells of the body and delivers its load. After unloading, the blood takes on waste products produced by the cells and carries them away for disposal. The body repeats the cycle, over and over, thousands of times a day. The engine that keeps this all going is the heart.

A Journey Through the Heart

The journey through the circulatory system begins as blood from the body enters the right atrium of the heart from two large veins, the superior **vena cava** and the inferior vena cava. The superior vena cava brings blood from the head and the arms. The inferior vena cava brings blood from the lower part of the body—the legs, pelvis, and abdomen. This blood, returning from its trip to the cells, carries carbon dioxide, a waste produced by the cells.

The Heart Cycle

The heart does its job of pumping by contracting, or squeezing, its chambers, just as someone can squirt water from a plastic bottle by squeezing its sides. But instead of a hand squeezing a bottle, the muscles of the heart compress the ventricles and atria.

The heart works in a three-part cycle, contracting twice, then resting briefly between each pair of contractions. This cycle is what causes the "lub-dub" sound that a doctor can hear when he or she listens to the heart. The two contractions and resting period make up one heartbeat.

The first part of the cycle, the resting period, is called **diastole**. During this period, blood from the body flows into the right atrium. At the same time, blood from the lungs flows into the left atrium.

When the atria are full, they compress, pushing their blood into the ventricles. This phase of the cycle, called **atrial systole**, creates the "lub" sound.

Blood in the right atrium flows through a one-way valve called the tricuspid valve into the right ventricle.

Blood in the left atrium flows through a one-way valve called the mitral valve into the left ventricle.

Now both ventricles compress, pushing blood out of the heart. This phase, which is called **ventricular systole**, causes the "dub" sound.

Blood in the right ventricle is pushed through another one-way valve called the pulmonary valve and into the lungs.

A person can also feel the heart beat. By putting a finger on the artery in the wrist or the neck, one can feel a pulsing sensation. This pulsing is caused by blood surging forward after each beat of the heart's ventricles.

diastole phase:

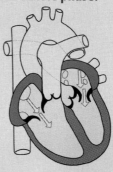

systole phase:

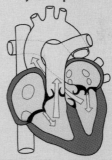

HEART CYCLES

Timing Is Everything

The heart's chambers must compress in a coordinated way to pump blood efficiently. The job of keeping this rhythm going falls to a group of cells in the heart called the **sinoatrial node**.[1] This node, also called a "natural pacemaker," sends out an electrical signal to the two atria. This signal tells the atria when to contract. After the atria contract, the signal travels on to the ventricles through special fibers in the heart's muscle. When the ventricles receive the signal, they contract.

The sinoatrial node's signals keep the heart beating in a regular rhythm. But sometimes the heart needs to beat faster. When a person exercises, the body's cells do more work. They need more oxygen and have more waste to get rid of. As a result, more blood needs to flow.

A part of the brain called the medulla oblongata gives the order to increase the heartbeat when more blood flow is needed. When a person is exercising or is under stress, the medulla oblongata sends out a signal that causes the sino-atrial node to transmit its signals faster. This causes the heart to beat more quickly.

In the Circuit

As blood leaves the heart and travels through the circulatory system, it flows into branches that grow smaller and smaller. Finally it reaches the network of tiny vessels that form a net or mesh called capillaries. The sides of these vessels are only one cell thick. The blood flows very slowly through this point. Here, the blood delivers its cargo of oxygen.

Oxygen molecules are packed into the capillaries. But at this point the surrounding cells contain much less oxygen. Passing through the thin capillary walls, the oxygen molecules travel from an area of high concentration (the oxygen-rich capillary) to an area of low concentration (the nearby cell). This process is called **diffusion**. At the same time, carbon dioxide created by the cells passes through the capillary wall and into the blood.

Other waste products from the cells also pass into the blood, which then continues through the capillaries and into the veins.

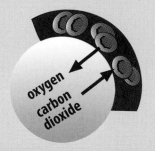

By now, the pressure from the heart is not strong enough to move the blood any further. Body muscles around the veins help to move the blood along as they compress and squeeze the vessels. In addition, the veins have one-way valves that keep the blood moving forward.

DIFFUSION
Molecules flow from an area of high concentration to one of low concentration. In this case, oxygen flows from capillaries to cells, while carbon dioxide flows from cells to capillaries.

Blood that was sent to the digestive system takes a slightly different route on the way back to the heart. This blood is sent to the liver. Here nutrients in the blood from digested food are absorbed and stored.

The liver also helps to clean the blood of any toxic substances. After leaving the liver, the blood is returned to the heart for another cycle.

Lymphatic System

Liquid surrounds all of the cells and tissues in the body. This liquid, called **interstitial fluid**, helps the body's cells move molecules to other cells and to the bloodstream. Too much interstitial fluid causes tissues to become swollen.

The lymphatic system prevents this problem. Lymphatic vessels are found in almost every tissue in the body. Like capillaries, they form a fine mesh of small tubes. Unlike capillaries, these tubes lead out of the tissues. Interstitial fluid flows into the lymphatic vessels. Once the fluid moves inside the lymphatic vessels, it is called lymph.

Like veins, the lymphatic vessels depend on movements of the surrounding muscles to help move the lymph.

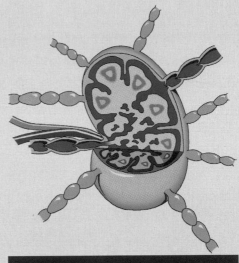

LYMPH NODE

The lymphatic system plays a major role in the body's immune system. The immune system fights bacteria, viruses, and other foreign invaders that might damage the body.

The immune system does much of its work in the lymph nodes. Here, white blood cells called lymphocytes quickly gather to fight infections. When foreign particles, such as bacteria, viruses, and fungi, enter the nodes, they are engulfed and destroyed by the lymphocytes.

When the body fights an infection, it can cause the lymph nodes to swell. This is because a large number of lymphocytes collect in the nodes.

After passing through the lymphatic system, the lymph is directed into the circulatory system through the right thoracic duct and the lymphatic duct.

Disease and Disorders

Diseases that affect the heart and circulatory system are called cardiovascular diseases. Cardiovascular diseases affect more than 82 million Americans. They are among the leading causes of death in the United States. In 2008, diseases of the heart and circulatory system caused almost one third of all deaths in the United States.[1]

Diseases of the Heart

Many cardiovascular diseases are caused by a condition called arteriosclerosis that causes artery walls to become thicker, harder, and less able to stretch. This can prevent blood from flowing where it needs to go. It can cause blockages in the heart's arteries.

Like any organ in the body, the heart needs a supply of blood so its cells can receive oxygen and nutrients. Three arteries called coronary arteries provide this blood. These arteries start at the aorta and branch into smaller arteries on the surface of the heart. If these arteries become blocked because of arteriosclerosis, the heart can be damaged.

Atherosclerosis is one type of arteriosclerosis. This disease is caused by a buildup of fatty deposits on the walls of the coronary arteries. This buildup can form a hard deposit called an atheroma. Atheromas can occur anywhere in the coronary artery, but they usually are found at places where the artery divides into smaller branches.[2] This condition is called coronary heart disease. If these arteries become blocked, the heart muscle cells that depend on the arteries won't receive enough oxygen.

A blockage can be caused by a slow buildup of deposits. A clot that forms in the artery can also cause a blockage. When the blockage is serious enough, a person may feel pain in his or her chest. This pain is called angina. It is a warning sign that the heart muscle is not receiving enough oxygen because the blood flow is blocked.

The cells in the heart's muscle use oxygen and nutrients to create the energy needed to pump the heart. When the muscle doesn't receive enough oxygen or nutrients, it must try other methods to create energy. These methods create waste products that cause pain when they are not removed from the cells.

An angina attack feels like something is gripping and squeezing the chest. The pain may also be felt in the back, the jaw, the shoulder, or the arm. People most often experience this pain when they exercise or are under stress. The pain usually goes away when the person rests.

Heart Attack

If a coronary artery becomes completely blocked, cells in the heart will die. This is called a heart attack or myocardial infarction. The severity of a heart attack depends on how much heart muscle dies.

The symptoms of a heart attack are similar to those of angina. In addition, the person may lose consciousness. In a severe heart attack, the heart may stop beating. This is called cardiac arrest. People in cardiac arrest will die if they are not treated within a few minutes.

Valve Problems

Many heart conditions are related to problems with the valves that control the flow of blood. Diseases or viruses can cause some of these problems. Other problems happen when the heart doesn't develop properly in a fetus.

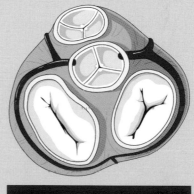

HEART VALVES

The valves of the heart are very important. If the valves do not work properly, blood may not flow through the heart the way it should, or the heart may not be able to pump blood efficiently. This affects the entire body.

Valve stenosis is a condition caused by valves that are too narrow and restrict blood flow through the heart. This condition can be caused by damage from some diseases, such as rheumatic fever, or by aging.

Valve incompetence is a condition caused by a valve that doesn't close completely. This can allow blood to flow backward through the heart. The faulty valve forces the heart to work harder to pump blood through the body. This condition can be caused by some infections and by coronary heart disease.

Congenital and Genetic Problems

When a fetus first begins developing, its heart looks like a simple tube. During a period of five weeks, this tube develops into a complex, four-chambered organ. Sometimes something goes wrong during this process. A hole can appear where one doesn't belong. An artery or vein may not develop in the right place, or a valve

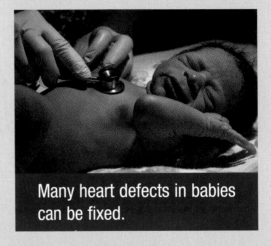

Many heart defects in babies can be fixed.

may not work properly. These problems that a baby is born with are called **congenital defects**. They occur in six to eight out of one thousand babies.[3] Many times these defects can be fixed by surgery.

Scientists aren't certain what causes these problems. In some cases, a virus in the mother may cause the damage. It is also possible that factors in the environment, such as certain chemicals, cause these defects. Some believe that these defects may be linked to a person's genes—the material in cells that people inherit from their parents. Genes determine our traits and sometimes the disorders we get.

Arrhythmias

In a normal person, the heart beats between sixty to one hundred times a minute in a regular cycle. The heart beats faster during times of exercise or stress. The rate slows once the person is resting.

Some diseases and conditions affect the heart rate, making it too slow, too fast, or erratic. Other conditions can cause the different parts of the heart to beat out of order. These conditions are called arrhythmias and can make the person experiencing them feel dizzy, have breathing problems, or suffer chest pain. In some cases the person can lose consciousness. Some rhythm disorders can be caused by other heart diseases, such as coronary artery disease.

Diseases of the Muscle and Tissue

Some diseases affect the heart muscle but are not caused by blocked arteries. Rheumatic fever or an infection from a virus can lead to myocarditis, a swelling of the heart muscle. Exposure to chemicals, drugs, or radiation can also cause this disorder.

Cardiomyopathy changes the structure of the ventricles or reduces their ability to pump blood. Vitamin or mineral deficiencies or excessive alcohol use can cause this disorder. It can also be inherited.

The pericardium is a tough membrane that surrounds and helps to protect the heart. Pericarditis is a swelling of the pericardium. This condition can cause a person to feel tired, have trouble breathing, or have a fever. This can be caused by an infection from a virus or by a heart attack. Other causes include kidney failure, cancer, tuberculosis, and physical injury.

Congestive heart failure is a condition in which the heart cannot pump enough blood through the body. It can be caused by a number of diseases and is most common in older people. This condition can cause coughing, fatigue, and a buildup of fluid in the body.

Diseases of the Circulatory System

Some diseases or conditions interfere with the circulatory system's ability to transport blood. Thrombosis causes a blood clot to form in a vessel. This clot can prevent blood from flowing through the vessel to organs and tissues. A clot, or thrombus, can develop where a blood vessel wall is damaged. Platelets in the blood stick to the site. These platelets release chemicals that trap other platelets and form a clot. If the clot grows large enough, it can completely block the blood vessel.

In some cases, a clot will break loose and move along the bloodstream. It will travel until it comes to an artery that is too small for it to pass through. Then it becomes stuck and blocks the flow of blood. This is called an embolism. If an embolism occurs in the lungs, it will prevent the lungs from getting enough blood and can cause death.

An embolism that occurs in the brain can damage parts of the brain that do not receive enough oxygen. This is called a cerebrovascular accident, or stroke.

Sometimes the wall of a blood vessel becomes weak. The force of the blood flowing through the vessel can cause it to bulge. This is called an aneurysm. An aneurysm that breaks can cause bleeding inside the body. If the bleeding is severe, a person can die.

Defective valves in the veins in the lower legs cause a condition known as varicose veins. The leaky valves allow blood to flow backward and collect in veins near the surface of the leg. This causes the veins to swell and appear as blue lines on the skin.

High Blood Pressure

When the heart pumps, it forces blood through the arteries and arterioles of the circulatory system. If these vessels become blocked or if they cannot expand to absorb the force of the heart's pumping, it will cause the body's blood pressure to rise above normal levels.

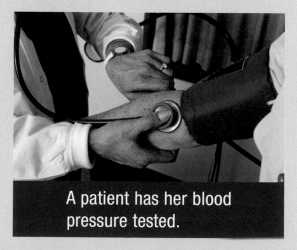

A patient has her blood pressure tested.

This condition is called high blood pressure, or hypertension. It is one of the most common diseases of the circulatory system, affecting about 50 million Americans. While hypertension can be measured and diagnosed, it often does not have any symptoms. If left untreated, it can increase the risk of other diseases and conditions, including stroke, heart attack, and kidney failure.

Diseases of the Blood

Anemia affects the ability of red blood cells to carry oxygen to other cells. People who are anemic may feel tired, weak, and lightheaded because their cells are not receiving enough oxygen.

They may also sweat a lot, have trouble breathing, and have a rapid heartbeat. Severe anemia can cause strokes and heart attacks.

Anemia can be caused by a lack of red blood cells or by damaged cells. This can be linked to poor diet, a disease such as cancer that destroys red blood cells, or an injury or condition that causes the loss of blood. Some people suffer from sickle cell anemia, a genetic disease that affects hemoglobin's ability to carry oxygen.

RED BLOOD CELLS
Normal on left; affected by sickle cell anemia on right

Bleeding disorders prevent blood from clotting when a blood vessel is damaged. Some of these disorders are caused by a lack of platelets in the blood. Others may result from platelets that don't stick to each other at the site of a damaged vessel. In other cases, a chemical that helps the clotting process may be missing or in short supply.

Other blood diseases affect the white blood cells that provide protection from viruses, bacteria, and infections. These diseases can damage existing white blood cells or reduce the bone marrow's ability to create new white blood cells. Some cancers, such as leukemia, damage the bone marrow, where white and red blood cells are created.

The spleen is an organ that helps to create, control, and destroy blood cells. Conditions that damage the spleen may lead to problems with blood cells. When the spleen grows larger because of disease or other condition, it traps more blood cells than normal. This can cause anemia and an increase in infections.

Diseases of the Lymphatic System

A disorder called lymphadenitis occurs when bacteria become trapped in lymph nodes. This causes the nodes to swell and become painful. A related condition called lymphangitis causes lymphatic vessels to swell and produces a fever or chills. Lymphadenopathy is a swelling in a lymph node caused by a nearby infection.

Lymphomas are cancers of the lymphatic system. This cancer causes lymphocytes—a type of white blood cell—to grow out of control. The affected lymphocytes may appear in one node or throughout the lymphatic system. Other cancers may also affect the lymphatic system. Cancerous cells may migrate or spread from their original source. Their route often takes them through the lymphatic system. Because of this, surgeons who operate on cancerous tumors often remove lymphatic vessels and nodes to stop the spread of the cancer.

Tonsillitis is one of the most common infections that affect the lymphatic system. The tonsils are a collection of lymphatic tissue in the back of the mouth. If a virus or bacteria infect the tissue, it can result in a sore throat and high fever and make it difficult to swallow. If the tonsils become infected too often, doctors may remove them.

Staying Healthy

Today doctors have many methods to help diagnose diseases of the heart and the circulatory system. Special scanning machines, radioactive dyes, and electrical sensors can all be used to determine the exact nature of a problem.

But before using such equipment, a doctor begins with a physical examination and a discussion with the patient. The doctor asks the patient a lot of questions. First, he or she asks about the patient's symptoms, such as chest pain or shortness of breath. The doctor also asks about the patient's medical history—what illnesses he or she may have had in the past. Information about the patient's family is also important, especially if a relative has had heart disease. According to the American Heart Association, people whose family members have heart disease are more likely to suffer heart disease themselves.

Then the doctor examines the patient. He or she checks to see if the patient is overweight. The doctor also looks at the patient's general appearance. For example, if the patient's skin has a bluish color, it may mean the cells are not getting enough oxygen.

The doctor measures the patient's blood pressure using a blood pressure cuff, or sphygmomanometer. High blood pressure is a sign of circulatory system disease and can also lead to other disorders. The doctor also checks the patient's pulse and feels the patient's chest to check for unusual vibrations. The doctor may tap the patient's chest. If the tapping produces a hollow sound, it means the patient's lungs are filled with air, which is good. If the sound is different, it can mean the lungs contain fluid.

The doctor uses a stethoscope to listen to the patient's heart. This device helps the doctor hear any unusual sounds that can mean problems with heart valves or abnormal blood flow.

After the physical examination is complete, the doctor decides if more tests are needed to determine the cause of the patient's problem. If so, there are plenty of options.

Electrocardiography

Electrocardiography is one of the more common tests doctors use to help uncover heart disease. This test measures the electrical pattern of the heart. To perform the test, the doctor places wires on the skin of the chest, the arms, and the legs. The wires pick up the heart's electrical signals, which are recorded in a machine that also prints them on a piece of paper.

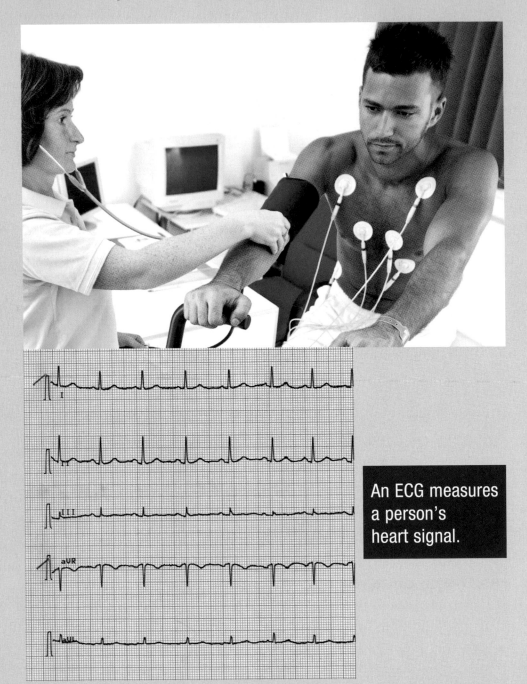

An ECG measures a person's heart signal.

The printout is called an electrocardiogram, or ECG or EKG. An electrical pattern that isn't normal can signal a problem, such as an arrhythmia or poor blood supply.

This test can be done while the patient is resting and while he or she is exercising. Some problems may not appear when the patient is at rest. In an exercise test, the patient walks on a treadmill or rides a stationary bicycle while attached to the ECG machine.

Some patients may have to wear a portable ECG machine for a day. This machine is called a Holter monitor. It runs on a battery and records patients' heart signals while they go about their daily routine. Patients record in a diary their symptoms and when they occur. The doctor uses the machine's recordings and the diary to track down problems.

Taking a Look Inside

Doctors have many different ways of viewing the heart and circulatory system without surgery. One way is to use a chest X-ray. This device shows the shape and size of the heart and also the outline of blood vessels in the lungs. It can also show if there is fluid in the lungs.

A more sophisticated form of X-ray is called computed tomography (CT) scanning. This method uses a computer to create three-dimensional pictures from a series of X-ray photos. A CT scan can reveal problems with the heart structure and the pericardium.

One widely used method for examining the heart and chest is echocardiography. This method uses high-frequency sound waves to create a picture of the internal organs. A device placed on the chest emits the sound waves, which cannot be heard by human ears. The sound waves bounce off the heart and other structures in the chest and are recorded by another device. A computer then uses this information to create a picture of the heart and the chest area.

Another kind of scanning technology, magnetic resonance imaging (MRI), uses a powerful magnet to create a picture of the heart and the chest. Because this technology costs a lot to operate, doctors do not often use it to diagnose circulatory system problems.

Is the Highway Clear?

To examine the circulatory system, doctors can inject a radioactive substance into the bloodstream through a vein. This substance can be detected by a special camera and allows doctors to find areas of the circulatory system that are blocked. This technique is called radionucleid imaging.

A type of radionucleid imaging called coronary angiography is used to find blockages in arteries. The medical team inserts a long, thin tube called a catheter into the patient's artery in the arm or the leg. The catheter is guided through the artery to the coronary arteries of the heart. When the catheter is in place, the doctor uses it to inject a special dye into the arteries. This dye can be seen on an X-ray camera and reveals where arteries may be blocked.

Catheters can also be used to put special instruments inside the heart. These instruments can measure blood pressure and flow.

Treatments

The simplest treatment for many heart and circulatory system diseases is prevention. Medical experts advise people to exercise and to eat a balanced diet. They recommend that patients eat less fat and don't smoke. People with high blood pressure may need to take medication for their condition.

Prevention doesn't always work, however. Even people who eat healthy foods and get plenty of exercise can still have heart disease. If a person develops heart or circulatory problems, doctors can use a variety of techniques to repair damage to the heart and the circulatory system. In some cases, doctors may even perform a heart transplant.

Coronary Artery Disease

Medications and surgery can be used to treat coronary artery disease. In some cases, a patient can take medicines that help to improve blood flow through the arteries. These drugs cause the arteries to expand, allowing blood to flow more freely. Patients may also take medicines that reduce blood pressure by forcing the heart to beat more slowly. These kinds of drugs are often prescribed for patients who suffer angina.

In more serious cases of coronary artery disease, surgery may be required. In one type of surgery, called balloon angioplasty, doctors insert a tiny deflated balloon into a partially blocked artery. When the balloon reaches the blockage, doctors inflate it. The inflated balloon then presses the plaque against the sides of the artery and opens a larger channel for blood flow.

In some cases, a tiny tube of metal mesh called a stent is inserted into the artery after the balloon. This mesh can help hold the artery open and prevent the blockage from returning. This is one of the most common procedures for treating coronary artery disease.

Doctors are testing other methods for removing blockages in coronary arteries. Laser angioplasty uses a laser attached to the end of a catheter. Doctors guide the laser to the problem area, then use pulsating beams of light to vaporize the blockage. A similar method uses a special cutting tool that is guided to the blockage by a catheter. Once it reaches the blockage, the tool is spun at high speeds and used to grind the plaque into small pieces. This is called atherectomy.

Heart Surgery

A coronary artery bypass can also be used to treat a blockage. This procedure creates a new route for the blood to flow to the heart. In this procedure, doctors put the patient to sleep, then cut through the breastbone in the center of the chest to reach the heart. The doctors must also cut through the pericardium.

Once the heart is exposed, doctors attach the patient to a machine that takes over the heart's job of circulating and oxygenating the blood. After this is done, doctors stop the heart with a chemical injection. Then the doctors remove a piece of vein from the patient's leg and attach it to the aorta. The other end of the vein is attached to the coronary artery below the blockage. More than one artery may be bypassed in a single operation.

In some cases, the surgeon is able to operate on the heart by making several small holes in the chest. Instruments, including a tiny camera, are inserted in the holes, and the surgeon performs the bypass without cutting open the patient's chest.

Valve Disorders

If one or more of the heart's valves are damaged badly enough, they may need to be replaced. Doctors can use either manufactured valves or valves from natural tissues. Manufactured valves are made from metal and plastic. They will last a long time but can cause blood to clot. Patients who receive manufactured valves have to take anti-clotting medicines for the rest of their lives.

Natural valves can be transplanted from other hearts. Some of these hearts come from people who have died and have asked that their organs be donated. Other valves come from the hearts of pigs, which are similar in structure to human hearts.

Surgery may also be used to correct other problems with the heart structure, including congenital defects.

Rhythm Disorders

A device called a pacemaker can help keep the heart beating steady if its natural pacemaker fails to work properly. A pacemaker sends out electrical signals through wires that are attached to the heart. These signals help to regulate the heart's rhythm.

Pacemakers are powered by batteries and are implanted into the body just below the skin. Some pacemakers send out regular signals; others work only when the heart begins beating erratically.

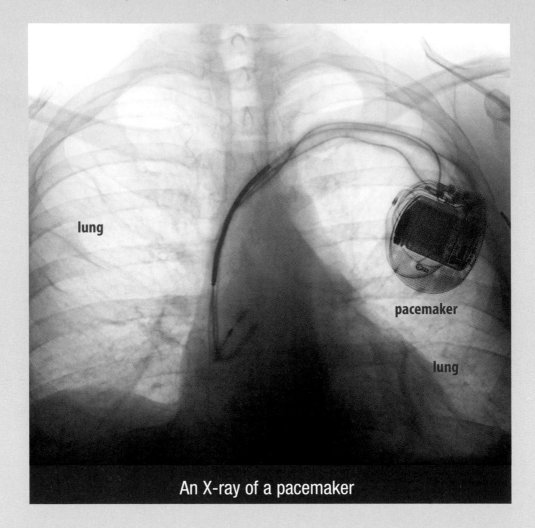

lung

pacemaker

lung

An X-ray of a pacemaker

In some cases, medicine may be used to keep the heart beating regularly. Substances that affect the way electrical impulses are passed through the heart may help to correct some kinds of arrhythmias. These medicines are called calcium channel blockers and cardiac glycosides.

Congestive Heart Failure

When a patient is suffering from heart failure, doctors try to make it easier for the heart to do its job. The patient can take medicines that expand blood vessels and allow the heart to pump with less force. Other drugs help the heart pump more efficiently and also reduce the amount of fluid in the body.

Heart Transplants

In cases of severe heart disease, doctors may decide to replace the patient's heart. This is a complicated operation. As in a bypass operation, the patient must be put to sleep and his or her chest opened. Doctors remove the diseased heart and insert the replacement heart. After the operation, the patient must take special medicines to prevent the body from rejecting the new heart.

Hearts for transplants come from the bodies of people who have died from causes other than heart disease.

Scientists are also working to build an artificial heart. The first artificial heart was implanted in 1982 in a man named Barney Clark. The device was called the Jarvik-7. Barney Clark lived for 112 days with the machine before he died.

Although a breakthrough at the time, the Jarvik-7 had several problems. Its pumping motion caused blood to clot. The device ran by compressed air that came from hoses attached to a 375-pound machine. This didn't offer much freedom for the patients who had to use the device. Doctors now use a modern version of the device, the Syncardia Total

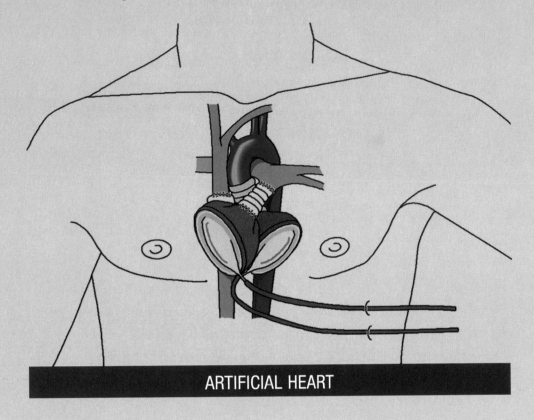

ARTIFICIAL HEART

Artificial Heart, to help keep patients alive while they wait for a heart transplant. However, it is not considered an option as a replacement heart.

More recently, researchers developed a device that can be implanted without a large external machine. The AbioCor Implantable Replacement Heart uses external batteries for its power. This device was first implanted in a seventy-one-year-old man in September 2001. The man lived for seventeen months before dying when part of the artificial heart failed. The company continues to offer the device for patients who are not suitable candidates for a heart transplant.

Future Study

Because diseases of the cardiovascular system affect so many people, scientists have spent a great deal of time studying the causes of these diseases. One of the longest running studies of circulatory system diseases is the Framingham Study. This project began in 1948 when researchers recruited more than five thousand men and women who lived in Framingham, Massachusetts, to participate in the study. The study's goal was to find the causes of cardiovascular diseases.

The researchers interviewed all the participants about their lifestyles and diets and put them through physical examinations. Then, every two years, they have examined and tested the members of the group. Through information gathered in this study, researchers have been able to find many causes of cardiovascular disease and identify risk factors that make it more likely that someone will have cardiovascular disease. The study continues today with many of the original members, as well as some of their children.

Amazing but True

The heart is an amazing organ. Even before a person is born it beats, and it keeps on beating until a person dies. On the average, the heart beats seventy times a minute. That's 100,000 times a day. During that time, it will pump 2,000 gallons of blood. Except in cases of medical intervention, the heart never stops beating while a person lives.

Cardiovascular disease has been the leading killer of Americans every year but one since 1900.[1]

In 2008, diseases of the heart and the circulatory system caused or contributed to the deaths of more than 800,000 Americans. These diseases directly caused almost 2,200 deaths a day or one death every thirty-nine seconds. Nearly 150,000 of those who died were under the age of sixty-five.[2]

After a person's body has fought an infection, the lymphocytes remember how to make the antibodies needed to fight the infection again.

More women than men die from cardiovascular disease. Of those who died in 2008, 52 percent were women and 48 percent were men.[3]

FILL 'ER UP: The body contains about ten pints of blood.

One in three adult Americans has high blood pressure. High blood pressure is called the "silent killer" because it can cause several diseases but has no symptoms of its own.[4]

WORLD'S LONGEST HIGHWAY
The circulatory system in the body is longer than any highway in the world. In fact, if all the arteries, veins, and capillaries were linked together, the path that resulted would cover more than 60,000 miles. That's long enough to go around the world twice with a little left over.

Chapter Notes

Chapter Two: Working Together

1. Charles Clayman, M.D., ed., *The Human Body: An Illustrated Guide to Its Structure, Function and Disorders* (New York: DK Publishing Inc., 1995), p. 104.
2. Philip Whitfield, *The Human Body Explained: A Guide to Understanding the Incredible Living Machine* (New York: Henry Holt and Company, 1995), p. 124.
3. Clayman, p. 108.
4. Whitfield, p. 126.
5. Clayman, p. 104.

Chapter Three: How Do the Systems Work?

1. Charles Clayman, M.D., ed., *The Human Body: An Illustrated Guide to Its Structure, Function and Disorders* (New York: DK Publishing Inc., 1995), p. 106.

Chapter Four: Disease and Disorders

1. *Heart Disease and Stroke Statistics—2012 Update: A Report from the American Heart Association,* American Heart Association, 2011 <http://circ.ahajournals.org/content/early/2011/12/15/CIR.0b013e31823ac046> (January 25, 2012).
2. Charles Clayman, M.D., ed., *The Human Body: An Illustrated Guide to Its Structure, Function and Disorders* (New York: DK Publishing Inc., 1995), p. 110.

3. Bernard J. Gersh, MD., ed., *The Mayo Clinic Heart Book*, 2nd Edition (New York: William Morrow, 2000), p. 59.

Chapter Six: Amazing but True

1. *Heart Disease and Stroke Statistics—2012 Update: A Report from the American Heart Association*, American Heart Association, 2011, <http://circ.ahajournals.org/content/early/2011/12/15/CIR.0b013e31823ac046> (January 25, 2012)

2. Ibid.

3. Ibid.

4. Ibid

Glossary

anemia—A condition marked by an insufficient number of red blood cells, or red blood cells that are unable to carry enough oxygen for the body's needs.

antibody—A protein that fights viruses and bacteria.

aorta—The major blood vessel directly attached to the heart's left ventricle.

arteries—Vessels that carry blood away from the heart.

arteriole—The smallest artery.

atrial systole—The phase of the heartbeat marked by the compression of the atria; causes the "lub" sound.

atrium—One of two topmost chambers of the heart, which receive blood from the veins.

capillaries—Tiny blood vessels with walls one cell thick that allow oxygen and nutrients to pass from blood into the body's cells.

cell—The smallest structure in the body capable of performing life processes.

circulatory system—The network of vessels that distribute blood, nutrients, and fluids throughout the body.

congenital defect—Damage to an organ or body structure that appears at birth.

diastole—The point in the heartbeat when the heart muscle relaxes, producing the lowest level of blood pressure.

diffusion—A chemical process in which molecules of a substance move from an area of high concentration to an area of low concentration.

erythrocytes—Red blood cells, the most numerous kind of blood cell in the body.

heart—A muscular organ that pumps blood and other fluids through the circulatory system.

hemoglobin—A protein carried by red blood cells that attaches to oxygen molecules, allowing oxygen to travel to body cells.

interstitial fluid—Fluid found between the cells of the body.

lymph—A fat-filled fluid found in the vessels of the lymphatic system.

lymphatic system—A network of vessels that collects excess fluid from body tissues and returns it to the circulatory system. It also plays a role in the body's immune response.

lymph node—A widening of the lymphatic vessel filled with a mesh-like tissue in which white blood cells collect.

pericardium—A tough membrane that surrounds and helps to protect the heart.

sinoatrial node—A collection of cells in the heart that sends electrical impulses to control the rhythm of the heartbeat.

thoracic duct—A large passage from which lymph drains from the lymphatic system into the veins.

thrombocyte—A type of white blood cell.

tunica adventitia—The outermost layer of cells in an artery.

tunica intima—The innermost layer of cells in an artery.

tunica media—The middle muscular layer of cells in an artery.

veins—Vessels that carry blood to the heart and the lungs.

vena cava—One of two large veins that channel blood into the heart's atria from the veins.

ventricle—One of two muscular chambers of the heart. The ventricles are the lower chambers.

ventricular systole—The phase of the heartbeat marked by the compression of the ventricles; causes the "dub" sound.

Further Reading

Books

Bjorklund, Ruth. *Circulatory System*. New York: Marshall Cavendish
    Benchmark, 2009.

Burstein, John. *The Amazing Circulatory System: How Does My Heart
    Work*? New York: Crabtree Pub. Co., 2009.

Corcoran, Mary K. *The Circulatory Story*. Watertown, Mass.
    Charlesbridge, 2010.

Parker, Steve. *Circulatory System*. Mankato, Minn. New Forest Press/
    Black Rabbit Books, 2011.

Internet Addresses

National Institutes of Health. NIH Heart, Lung and Blood Institute.
<http://www.nhlbi.nih.gov>

Nemours. KidsHealth.
<http://www.kidshealth.org>

Index